Working Paper 62

JAVANESE MARKETS REVISITED

by

Glen Chandler

Published by
The Centre of Southeast Asian Studies
Monash University
Clayton
Victoria
Australia 3168

National Library of Australia
ISBN 0 7326 0196 7
ISSN 0314 6804

1990

JAVANESE MARKETS REVISITED

My first impression on returning to the village markets in D.I. Yogyakarta which were the focus of my research nine years earlier (Figure 1) was that little had changed. Familiar faces greeted me from behind stock that was almost identical to that carried before. Women still sat surrounded by fruit and vegetables, handicraft traders stood by their piles of tikar (woven grass matting), or among baskets and conical hats. Men attended to song birds in cages loaded one upon the other on the rear of their bicycles or sat behind their sewing machines waiting for work. Women continued to line the pathways of the marketplaces sitting behind baskets of bean curd, cakes or peanuts while young men stood at the intersections of the pathways with plastic trays displaying a variety of manufactured goods. But behind the familiar sights and sounds some changes had occurred.

This paper explores three types of changes that have occurred in the village markets since my original research was conducted in 1979 (Chandler, 1979) and 1980 (Chandler, 1981, 1984, 1985). The most visible changes to occur are seen in the upgrading of the market facilities to provide better conditions for both the traders and customers. Secondly, there have been some significant changes in the distribution channels behind some consumer durables which demonstrate that the formal sector of the economy is playing a greater role in the village marketplaces. Finally, I shall discuss the changes that have occurred with respect to the composition of the trader population and the range of goods sold.

Before tackling the changes that have occurred in the marketplaces though, it is worth mentioning that there have been significant changes to the transport system in the study area since 1980. In this context it is not necessary to explore those changes in detail, but just to mention a few salient points.

West of the Yogyakarta-Magelang road the only transport operating during 1980 went via Sleman, passing by Cebongan to go through Seyegan and Balangan to Kebonagung. Colts still use this route, during the mornings there are several departures every hour from Yogyakarta. Colts also now go from the main road direct to Kebonagung via Cebongan. Whilst this route was open in 1979 it was closed during 1980 because the bridge just beyond Cebongan had collapsed and the repairs had not been completed before my fieldwork was finished. However the departure times of Colts using this route are now far apart - sometimes an hour or more elapses (which was a rare occurrence before) - and this is because the villagers living along this route often prefer to use the 'Pemuda' bus service which takes a route from Yogyakarta via Godean, through Seyegan and Gendol to Tempel. Those living in this area are now much better served with public transport than before, not only in greater comfort as the

Figure 1

LOCATION OF STUDY MARKETS

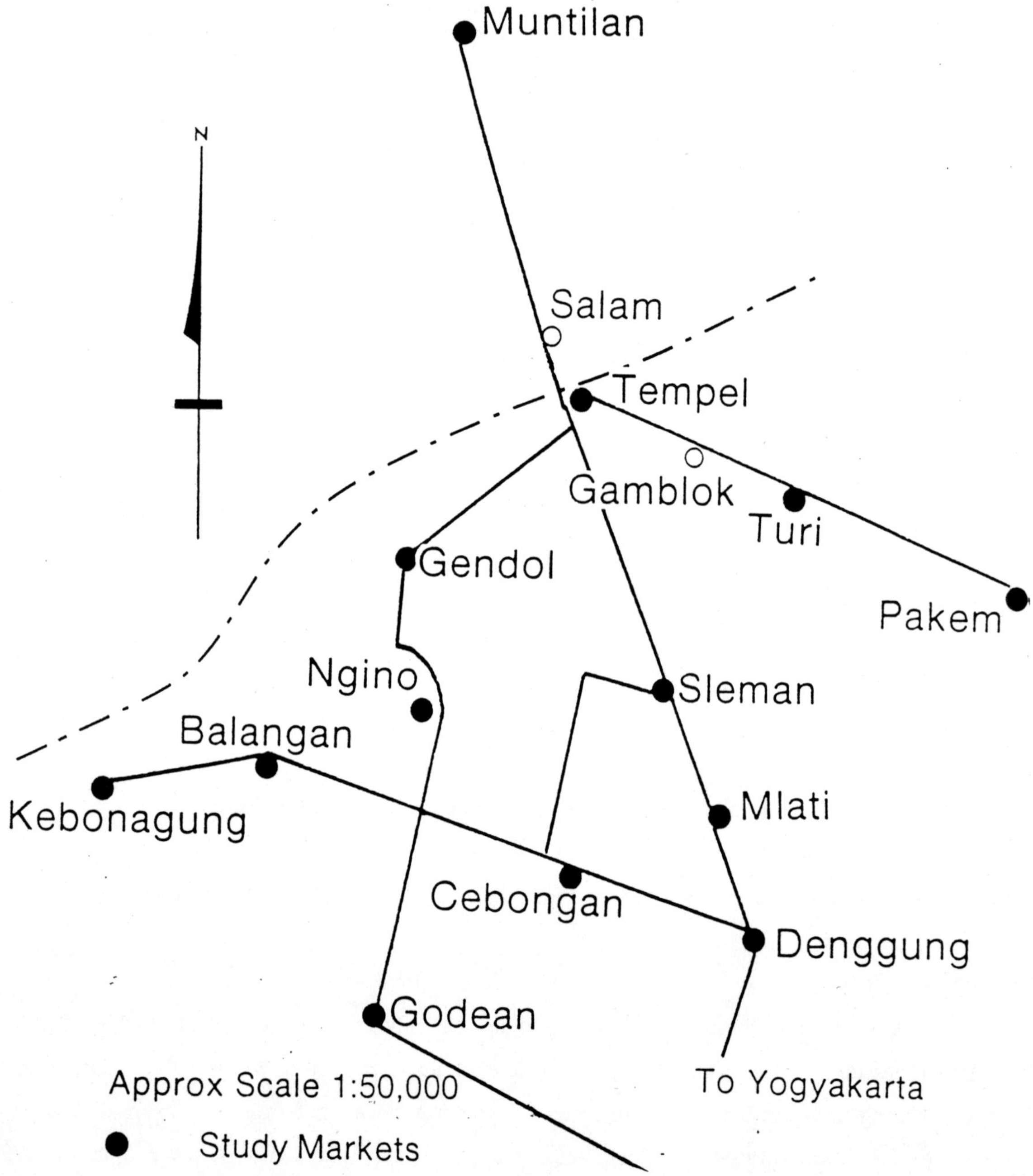

Approx Scale 1:50,000

● Study Markets

○ Markets on which no data was collected

—— Road

— · — Boundary between the provinces of D.I. Yogyakarta and Central Java

Source: Compiled from field notes using maps supplied by Universitas Gadjah Mada, Yogyakarta.

overcrowding that was all too evident before no longer exists, but also because they now, in many cases, have a choice of route. People in Seyegan in 1980 could only go to Yogyakarta via Sleman; now they may take a more direct route via Godean. Because there are more public transport routes more villagers now have access to buses or Colts. This may well affect their shopping habits and may even mean their dependence on local markets may not be as great as before. This subject would, of course, make a great research topic!

The public transport service between Tempel and Pakem, taking in Turi, is also greatly improved. During 1980 it was not unusual for me to give up trying to reach Turi from Tempel or Pakem after waiting for over an hour. There were plenty of Colts when it was market day at Turi but at other times the service was dreadful. Nowadays 'Pemuda' buses compete with the Colt service and people living along this route are much better served; the waiting time in 1989 was seldom more than five minutes.

Transport through the study area using the main Yogyakarta-Magelang road has remained the same with Colts stopping along the route where passengers wait to be picked up or wish to be dropped off. The large buses make few stops and anyone who wishes to make a shorter journey than to Tempel is direct to the Colts.Physical changes to the marketplaces

These markets in 1980 gave the appearance of having evolved over a period of time. Increased numbers of traders meant new additions were made to the marketplace in order to accommodate them. The layout was often a confused jumble of pathways with the customer having to negotiate a number of turns in order to reach a particular section of the marketplace. In the absence of sufficient raised platforms some traders built their own from bamboo to accommodate their goods and themselves.

While there was some variation between and within the marketplaces, traders selling consumer durables and a variety of foodstuffs were usually accommodated on one of a number of raised concrete platforms with tiled roofing supported by wooden posts planted either in the dirt pathways or in the concrete. Because the roofing did not extend across the pathways those traders seated on the ground were not protected from sun or rain. And, as the morning progressed even some of the traders seated on the platforms had to tie pieces of cloth over the gaps to protect themselves from the harsh sun. (Refer to Chandler, 1979:44-52 for a more detailed description of the physical characteristics of these marketplaces.) Conditions for those on the platforms were, however, adequate. But for those seated on the ground improvement would have doubtless been welcomed.

One of the first markets I visited on my return was Cebongan which had undergone a facelift with the entire marketplace having been rebuilt. (Refer Chandler, 1979:38 for an illustration of what part of Cebongan looked like prior to the renovations.) New raised concrete platforms for the traders, concrete pathways and new corrugated iron roofing which was designed to keep the rain out of the whole area and allow some light to filter through, have meant the traders and their customers are better protected from the weather and can operate in more comfortable conditions. Those walking in the new marketplace will no longer experience the slippery conditions which accompany rain. The new constructions are not merely upgrading the existing platforms using the old marketplace layout. In the case of Cebongan the whole marketplace has been transformed with a regular grid pattern of pathways. Renovations using the same style of construction are under way at Sleman, Tempel and Pakem . In these markets at the moment traders are crammed into other parts of the marketplace while work is in progress. As far as I could ascertain these markets, too, will be laid out in a uniform grid pattern.

Where the renovations have been carried out not all stallholders benefit. Many of the traders at Cebongan continue to trade in the open air in front of the new buildings. There has been no attempt to accommodate all traders; the authorities are no doubt aware that many traders prefer not to occupy a concrete stall space as the market fee charged is higher (usually double) and their enterprise is too small. The new renovations have meant that the atmosphere of the markets remains the same but conditions are much improved for those who prefer to be under cover.

I was informed by some traders that renovations will also be made to Godean and Ngino markets. There was no indication that similar work will be carried out at Turi, a market which does deserve some attention in this respect. The smaller markets of Gendol, Balangan and Kebonagung, all with older-style constructions, are probably not on the agenda for some time.

The small market at Mlati in 1980 consisted of a number of traders lining a small roadway (Chandler, 1984:24, 1979:49). The construction of a marketplace for these stallholders (quite distinct in design from the larger markets) could be one reason the number of traders in this market has doubled. Whereas in 1980 there were between sixty and eighty traders in attendance on any particular day (Chandler, 1984:192), this number has now increased to more than 130. The new marketplace is not full and some traders prefer to sit by the roadside as before because (a) the position is more prominent than the available spaces at the rear of the new market building, and (b) the market fee charged is less than applies for those traders sitting under cover.

Of course the money to finance the market rebuilding program has to come from somewhere. There is so indication that the renovations are being subsidised by the traders in increased daily market fees. Traders throughout the area, whether in the renovated markets or not, are paying considerably more for their stall space than previously. Whereas in 1980 a clothing trader paid Rp25 for stall space at Cebongan this has now increased to Rp100. Another trader, at Gendol, paid Rp25 in 1980 and now in 1989 pays Rp100. Likewise the dadung (twine) trader who at Tempel paid Rp50 in 1980 now pays Rp150 per day for his stall space. This increase seems to be out of proportion to other price increases over this period. For example a Colt ride from Yogyakarta to Sleman in 1980 cost Rp100 compared to Rp250 in 1989, and at a time when world fuel prices have risen dramatically.The distribution of consumer durables

In my 1980 research considerable emphasis was placed on the channels of distribution behind a number of consumer durables sold in the village markets (Chandler, 1980, 1984). During this latest trip I was interested to note some changes had occurred in this aspect of marketing since that time.Plastic and rubber footwear

In 1980 rubber thongs and sandals were always purchased by the market traders from wholesalers located in either Yogyakarta or Magelang. Once in the marketplace there was no further wholesaling with, for example, one trader selling to another at a discounted price. In contrast to the situation with clothing sold in the markets (Chandler, 1984:119-42) there were no wholesalers operating in the village markets. The distribution pattern pertaining to footwear was strictly hierarchical and this feature I attributed to (a) a limited number of sources of supply and (b) the non-existence of small-scale intermediaries bypassing the wholesale outlets by purchasing direct from the manufacturer and selling direct to the mobile traders. There were clearly insufficient retail traders selling footwear in these markets to provide and adequate living for an intermediary (1984:78-9).

By 1989 the number of footwear traders had not increased. If anything, the numbers were slightly lower than before with several male traders who once sold a few rubber thongs in addition to their main stock of, for example, posters and calendars, no longer doing so. However, many of the traders I spoke with during my last visit claimed to be purchasing some, or all, of their replacement stock of footwear in the marketplaces.

At Godean market I met a man who, with his stock of footwear in the rear of a small van, was approaching traders with his wares. According to this man he has been selling footwear wholesale for approximately one year now and he purchases his stock from Yogyakarta. He attends the markets on their market days when footwear traders (who usually sell in several markets over the five-day Javanese market week) are in attendance. This man regularly visits Godean, Sleman, Tempel, Pakem, Turi, Gendol, Balangan and Ngino markets (refer Figure 1). Although this man has only been selling for one year conversations with footwear traders indicate that this type of wholesaling may have been going on for about five years.

Given that many of the retail footwear traders I spoke with continued to purchase all or some of their replacement stock from either Yogyakarta or Magelang, I was curious as to how the wholesaler earned sufficient income. However, in addition to selling to the market traders he also sells to shops in the villages, and it is this participation in both the formal and informal sectors of the economy which provides him with a living. Furthermore, it is apparent that the sales to market traders form only a small part of his business.

At this point it is worth noting that nearly all the villages I visited boasted several more shops than previously. And, in many cases, the range of stock was wider than before and also a little more 'up-market', suggesting that more village people than before are patronising shops for some of their consumer durables. A few shops have even introduced dummies for displaying frocks, a feature earlier confined to shops in Yogyakarta itself. It is not, therefore, an increase in market trade which has facilitated the existence of the wholesaling of footwear in the village marketplaces but an increase in formal sector retailing at the village level.

Unfortunately I was unable to ascertain whether the profit margin on the footwear was identical for shopkeepers and market traders. It is possible that the wholesaler might have been able to sell with a higher mark-up to shopkeepers, thus increasing the profitability of his enterprise. As discussed previously (1984:28), consumer goods sold in shops are often more expensive than those sold in the marketplaces, and it is possible to assume the wholesaler might be able to charge more to shopkeepers.

I should mention at this stage that the range of stock carried by the wholesaler was comprehensive. There was no discernible difference in the displayed stock of those market traders who purchased from him and those who bought elsewhere. It cannot, therefore, be argued that wholesaling in the marketplaces has contributed to a wider range of footwear for the consumer, nor has it reduced the choice.

Several footwear traders in the market continued to buy all, or some of, their stock from their traditional suppliers in Yogyakarta or Magelang because they claimed they were cheaper. Others said the prices were the same. For those traders who purchase from Yogyakarta the wholesaler offers competitive prices. But he is dearer than the trader at Magelang where several traders go. One advantage of the wholesaler for the market traders is they can replenish their stock slowly instead of saving up to make a large enough purchase to cover the cost of travelling to Yogyakarta or, especially, Magelang (cf. Chandler, 1984:76-7).

The convenience of purchasing from a wholesaler may, in one respect, be more pronounced for shopkeepers than for market traders. While shops are generally open almost all day, market traders usually pack up their stalls around midday and are therefore free to travel to an alternative source of supply to buy replacement stock. In so doing they are not risking losing any sales. Shopkeepers, however, may find themselves with less free time to make such trips. The introduction of local wholesaling of footwear has probably made more difference to shopkeepers than market traders. In talking to the market traders I gained the distinct impression that wholesaling of footwear, while it was sometimes more convenient for them, was not that important. Given that most of the traders have been selling footwear for many years, longer than the existence of wholesaling in the marketplaces, this is not surprising. It is possible that as new traders enter the marketplaces to sell footwear they will be less inclined to travel to sources of supply, not having established the habit. In time a greater proportion of footwear traders may take advantage of the opportunity to purchase their stock locally, thus avoiding the need to travel to a source of supply, not only a time-consuming venture but also one that involves the outlay of money for fares.Kitchenware

While I did predict in 1984 (p.165) that wholesaling of footwear in the markets may take place some time in the future, I certainly did not anticipate that kitchenware, with its low turnover and high bulk, would be sold wholesale in much the same way.

In my 1980 research I discovered that almost all kitchenware traders purchased their stock from Yogyakarta, being regular customers at shops located in the streets adjacent to Pasar Beringharjo, such as 'Toko Liong', 'Sari Gelas', 'Juono' and 'Sari Warah'. The only traders who bought elsewhere were young men who specialised in one item of kitchenware (for example plastic ware and enamel basins) who purchased their stock direct from the manufacturer or from Magelang market (Chandler, 1984:85-6). The numbers of these latter traders have since declined dramatically; I suspect their enterprises have suffered because they overspecialised in an area where demand is too low (cf. Chandler, 1984:86).

I was certainly surprised to see a van at Tempel market one day, the rear of which was packed tightly with a wide range of the faster-moving kitchenware items. Naturally I approached the driver and subsequently learnt that this was a wholesale enterprise which was based in Jakarta but with branches throughout Java. The Yogyakarta branch has been operating for approximately eight years and has four vans on the road visiting various villages in the area. The company does not operate from a shop and therefore does not sell retail, nor may traders visit the office and purchase direct.

The kitchenware traders do not have to leave their stalls to buy from the wholesaler. He enters the marketplace to take orders and returns to his van parked in a side street to fetch the appropriate goods to take them to the traders. While this is more convenient for the traders, it does mean they do not in this way see a display of any new stock that may come on the market. However, while all kitchenware traders in the larger markets in the study area (cf. Chandler, 1984:35-41) buy stock from this wholesaler, few use him as their sole source of supply. By continuing to visit their traditional sources of supply they do come across new items they may consider will sell in the villages.

According to the kitchenware traders I spoke with, the prices charged by the visiting wholesaler are about the same as those charged by their traditional suppliers in the large stores located in the vicinity of Pasar Beringharjo. The kitchenware traders now have the advantage of being able to purchase the more popular stock items without incurring travelling costs. On their visits to Yogyakarta they may now concentrate on buy the goods not normally carried by the wholesaler.

In 1984 I noted (p.87) that the high transport costs, coupled with high capital investment in stock, necessary for the wholesale distribution of kitchenware would make such wholesaling an uneconomic proposition. My failure here was to assume that such wholesaling would be undertaken by the informal sector. I had envisaged an independent trader with limited credit using public transport or, at best, an unreliable vehicle, purchasing stock from the existing Yogyakarta wholesaling outlets and selling at a low profit margin to traders eager to save themselves the trouble and costs related to purchasing stock. This assumption regarding the scale of operations was related to my experience in the wholesaling of clothing in these same markets (Chandler, 1981, 1984:146-66). I certainly did not imagine that the wholesaling of kitchenware in these village markets might form a part of a wider distribution network managed, ultimately, from a head office in Jakarta. This type of wholesaling is another example of the involvement of the formal sector of the economy in the village marketplaces.

As is the case with the wholesaling of footwear discussed above, the wholesaling of kitchenware is not confined to the market traders. In addition to visiting marketplaces the kitchenware van also calls upon village shops. Given that many of the shops carry in their range some kitchenware items, there is little doubt that wholesaling to both the informal and formal sector outlets in the villages helps boost sales to a sufficient level to better cover the transport costs involved and therefore maintains viability of the wholesaling enterprise.Dadung twine

Dadung is a twine made from the bark of the Aren tree and is used mainly for tying lengths of bamboo together in house construction. It is also converted into brooms and dusters in cottage industry. During 1980 there was only a small amount of wholesaling of dadung and this occurred principally because of the overlapping itineraries of two dadung traders who sold it in a different form (a woman who sold the twine wound round two crossed sticks, and a man - Pak Hanan - who sold it in hanks). Every five days (on Paing) these two traders would sell at Sleman market and occasionally they would buy from each other at a wholesale price and take the new stock to other markets on their itineraries where it was not sold by any other trader in that form (Chandler, 1984:114-8). However, this woman has since withdrawn from trade and now the only dadung trader at Sleman market is Pak Hanan. Now that there are no overlapping itineraries at Sleman there is no longer the opportunity for wholesaling different varieties of dadung.

At other markets in the area, for example Cebongan, Godean and Ngino, several traders offer dadung on the major day. However in these cases the range of their stock is identical and there is, therefore, no point in buying wholesale in order to offer customers a greater choice.

The formal sector has not become involved in the wholesaling of dadung. This is no doubt because it continues to be woven as a cottage industry. Given that it is made up locally for a local market it is unlikely that the type of wholesaling which applies nowadays to footwear and kitchenware will occur with respect to dadung.Clothing

The combination of the hierarchical and horizontal forms of clothing distribution discussed in Chandler (1981, 1984) continues unchanged. Wholesalers who purchase their stock from Pasar Klewer in Solo still occupy stall space at the village markets on their major days, concentrating their sales on retail traders. Tailors approach both retail and wholesale traders in the markets with clothing they have sewn at home. Retail traders who do some sewing at home continue to sell to other retail traders. People who buy batik direct from factories still sell wholesale to traders in the markets. And most clothing traders still go to Pasar Beringharjo in Yogyakarta to replenish some of their stock. For a more complete discussion of this feature of market trade refer to Chandler (1984:104).

There is no evidence that the formal sector, that is someone with a van acting as a representative of a factory or clothing distribution concern, has moved into the village markets with clothing. Should this occur in the future with factory-made clothing it is likely that such wholesaling will coexist with informal sector wholesaling at the village level. This is because so much of the clothing available in the village markets is produced locally by the informal sector of the economy and is not easily incorporated into a central bulking enterprise. Locally-based tailors, therefore, will continue to visit their local marketplace in order to sell direct to the retail clothing traders.

Maybe it can be said that where wholesaling of consumer durables in these markets already exists (such as in clothing) that there is less room for the formal sector to profit. Furthermore, I would conclude from my observations that at present most of the clothing sold in these markets is produced by the informal sector (farming and street shorts, frocks, trousers, most children's clothing) rather than in factories (tee-shirts, bras, socks. Presumably as demand increases for the manufactured items there will be more opportunity for formal sector wholesaling in the village markets.Changes in the market trader **population**

During 1980 a census was conducted of the number of stalls functioning every day of the Javanese five-day market week in each of the markets in the study area (Chandler, 1984:185-98). In 1989, due to a time constraint, a more limited census was conducted. An attempt was made to visit each market on its major days only. As discussed previously (Chandler, 1984:30-4) it is the major day which is the most crowded and the one on which the widest variety of goods is offered. Unfortunately it was not possible to include Muntilan market and, as can be seen in Table 1, I was not able to visit the small markets of Gendol and Kebonagung on one of their major days. Nevertheless in comparing the figures from these two periods it is possible to identify changes that have occurred in the number of stalls in the markets.

Table 1 provides a comparison of the total number of stalls in the markets during 1980 and 1989 and gives a breakdown into whether the stalls are attended by females, males, or both. With respect to the relative sizes of these markets only one, Pakem on Pon, has grown appreciably over the nine-year period. However a closer look at the figures will reveal that there are still more traders at Pakem on Legi than on Pon and the increase can be seen to balance out the difference in size of the trader population between these two days. Quite a few markets have experienced a decline in the number of stalls. At Balangan the difference between the two major days of Legi and Wage is now not quite as pronounced since the decline in the number of traders present on Wage. There are also fewer traders at Ngino on Legi, but some of these could easily have transferred to nearby Balangan instead; Balangan experiencing a slight increase on Legi. There is also a decline in the number of stalls at Tempel on Wage and at Turi on both days. The decline in the number of traders at Godean is only slight (2.5 per cent) considering the size of this market in the first place.

There are some interesting figures in this table that deserve further exploration. As can be seen, on nine of the days that a census was conducted there has been a decline in the participation of women, some of this quite significant. If we look at Turi, for example, there are some interesting conclusions that may be drawn.

Table 1

No. of Stalls on Major Days

Market	Major Day	1980				1989				Difference in Total Nos.			
		Fem.	Male	Both	Total	Fem.	Male	Both	Total	Fem.	Male	Both	Total
Balangan	Legi	210	5	1	216	234	4	3	241	+24	-1	+2	+25
	Wage	365	10	7	382	307	16	4	327	-58	+6	-3	-55
Cebongan	Kliwon	391	85	6	482	408	91	8	507	+17	+6	+2	+25
Gendol	Paing	127	2	3	132	126	3	1	130	-1	+1	-2	-2
	Pon	122	1	1	124	*							
	Kliwon	138	5	-	143	111	5	1	117	-27		+1	-26
Godean	Pon	837	185	20	1042	776	218	22	1016	-61	+33	+2	-26
Kebonagung	Pon	257	24	1	282	241	20	5	266	-16	-4	+4	-16
	Kliwon	202	6	3	211	*							
Muntilan	Pon	1006	341	50	1397	*							
	Kliwon	955	339	39	1333	*							
Ngino	Legi	515	96	29	640	445	92	16	553	-70	-4	-13	-87
	Wage	471	113	7	591	485	105	16	606	+14	-8	+9	+15
Pakem	Legi	659	171	31	861	672	172	18	862	+13	+1	-13	+1
	Pon	486	58	8	552	575	72	16	663	+89	+14	+8	+111
Sleman	Paing	473	146	10	629	481	177	14	672	+8	+31	+4	+43
Tempel	Legi	512	99	13	624	512	105	13	630		+6		+6
	Wage	591	135	27	753	554	129	9	692	-37	-6	-18	-61
Turi	Paing	489	62	19	570	451	61	5	517	-38	-1	-14	-53
	Kliwon	572	71	12	655	475	82	5	562	-97	+11	-7	-93

* Figures not collected due to time constraint.

Source: Censuses conducted in 1980 (Chandler, 1984: 185-98) and 1989.

Table 2

Women operated stalls at Turi market

Year	Market Day	No. of stalls operated by women		
		Fruit/Veg	Home Prep. Food	Grain
1980	Paing	116	170	58
1989	Paing	105	128	23
	Difference:	-11	-42	-35
1980	Kliwon	148	170	58
1989	Kliwon	106	139	18
	Difference:	-42	-31	-40

Source: Market censuses conducted 1980 (Chandler, 1984:198) and 1989.

As can be seen above, the decline in the participation of women has been in the sale of foodstuffs, typically those requiring low capital investment and yielding poor profits. And their place is not being taken by men; my figures indicate that the number of male stallholders in these categories remain constant. It would appear that either the demand for these foodstuffs in Turi has declined or many of the traders are no longer willing to compete for the meagre profits that this small-scale trade brings (cf. Chandler, 1985).

At the same time there has been an influx of 89 women into Pakem marketplace on Pon, 34 of whom belong in these three same categories (refer to Table 3 below).

Table 3

Women operated stalls at Pakem market on Pon

Year	Stall Category		
	Fruit/Veg.	Home Prep. Food	Grain
1980	137	135	45
1989	158	158	47
Increase:	21	22	1

Source: Censuses conducted by Chandler 1980 (1984:195) and 1989.

As discussed above, the public transport between Tempel and Pakem - passing through Turi - has improved considerably since 1980. Because buses and Colts now pass through Turi every few minutes some women living in the environs of Turi must find it easier nowadays to travel to Pakem, a much busier market with a larger catchment area, to sell their produce.

But even if all of the 34 extra women selling in these categories in Tempel are from Pakem, it still means that in excess of 50 women who once sold in Turi market now no longer do so. And there has been almost no change in the participation rate of women in these three categories at Tempel market. An exploration of this issue would make an interesting research topic. Why have so many women stopped selling in Turi market (almost 17 per cent) and what, if any, alternative income-earning opportunities have they adopted?

It is interesting to note the increase in the number of stalls offering manufactured goods over this period of time. Focussing on the larger markets only (cf. Chandler, 1984:35-41) Table 4 shows that this category of trade has seen a tremendous influx of men. It must be noted one cannot add these figures to arrive at an overall total as most of these manufactured goods traders sell in several markets each five-day week and many would also sell in markets outside the study area. This table illustrates that the demand for such goods has, at all venues but Ngino, increase considerably and that it has been men who have been the quickest to respond.

Clearly the sale of these formal sector commodities (e.g. jewelry, calendars, footwear, books, plastic sheeting, kitchenware) has become more important in the markets in recent years, in fact has become a growth area. As in 1980 the availability of these goods remains much greater on major market days than on the minor days. As discussed previously (Chandler, 1984:64-7), where men move into market trade higher capital investment is usually required - and this is true for many of the manufactured goods sold. It seems more and more people, especially men, are becoming involved in the sale of formal sector goods in an informal sector environment - the marketplace.Conclusion

As is to be expected, market are dynamic places constantly undergoing a variety of changes in their physical, social and economic features. This paper has explored only some of the changes that have occurred over a nine-year period.

It is apparent that these markets are not being left behind by development. The physical structures have in many cases been upgraded with a concerted rebuilding program. Conditions for both the traders and the customers have, as a result, improved. The involvement of the formal sector in the wholesaling of some consumer durables, notably factory-made goods such as kitchenware and rubber thongs, has meant the marketplaces, traditionally associated with informal sector activities, are capable of adapting to formal sector marketing techniques. Likewise the formal sector is able to take advantage

Table 4

No. stalls selling manufactured goods on major days

Year	Market	Major Day	No. stalls Fem.	Male	Both	Total
1980	Cebongan	Kliwon	27	18	-	45
1989	"	"	25	31	-	56
			-2	+13		+11
1980	Godean	Pon	35	34	3	72
1989	"	"	39	54	7	100
			+4	+20	+4	+28
1980	Ngino	Legi	24	19	1	44
1989	"	"	15	26	1	42
			-9	+7	-	-2
1980	Ngino	Wage	24	16	2	42
1989	"	"	11	21	5	37
			-13	+5	+3	-5
1980	Pakem	Legi	22	20	3	45
1989	"	"	24	56	3	83
			+2	+36	-	+38
1980	Pakem	Pon	11	3		14
1989	"	"	12	27	3	42
			+1	+24	+3	+28
1980	Sleman	Paing	24	33	-	57
1989	"	"	24	56	2	82
			-	+23	+2	+25
1980	Tempel	Legi	41	20	2	63
1989	"	"	39	36	3	78
			-2	+16	+1	+15
1980	"	Wage	44	25	1	70
1989	"	"	41	40	2	83
			-3	+15	+1	+13
1980	Turi	Paing	11	6	3	20
1989	"	"	21	13	1	35
			+10	+7	-2	+15
1980	"	Kliwon	19	7	1	27
1989	"	"	20	22	-	42
			+1	+15	-1	+15

Source: Censuses conducted in 1980 (Chandler, 1984: 185-98) and 1989.

of informal marketing outlets. And, finally, it is clear that more and more retail traders are finding it worthwhile to offer manufactured goods in the marketplaces on their major days. While the demand for these goods is still such that they only need to be available on a periodic basis, that is the major days, it is clear that the demand is such that more traders are able to earn a living selling such goods in what has traditionally been regarded as the informal sector. The question here is whether this growth will continue in the future.

REFERENCES CITED

Chandler, G.N. 1979. Village Markets in D.I. Yogyakarta, Indonesia. B.A. Hons. thesis, Department Geography, Monash University.

Chandler, Glen. 1981. "Market traders and the sale of clothing in rural Java", Monash Centre of Southeast Asian Studies Working Paper 25.

Chandler, Glen. 1984. Market Trade in Rural Java. Monash Papers on Southeast Asia No. 11.

Chandler, Glen. 1985. "Rural Market Women in Java", Prisma 37:57-67